W9-AKY-558

THE TEACHER, TEACHER JOKE BOOK

Compiled and Edited by
JENNIFER HAHN

BARBOUR
PUBLISHING

THE
TEACHER,
TEACHER
JOKE BOOK

© 2004 by Barbour Publishing, Inc.

ISBN 1-59310-138-4

All rights reserved. No part of this publication may
be reproduced or transmitted for commercial pur-
poses, except for brief quotations in printed reviews,
without written permission of the publisher.

Churches and other non-commercial interests may
reproduce portions of this book without the express
written permission of Barbour Publishing, provided
that the text does not exceed 500 words or 5 per-
cent of the entire book, whichever is less, and that
the text is not material quoted from another publisher. When reproducing text from this book,
include the following credit line: "From *The Teacher,
Teacher Joke Book,* published by Barbour Publishing,
Inc. Used by permission."

Published by Barbour Publishing, Inc.,
P.O. Box 719, Uhrichsville, Ohio 44683 www.bar-
bourbooks.com

*Our mission is to publish and distribute inspirational
products offering exceptional value and biblical
encouragement to the masses.*

Member of the
Evangelical Christian
Publishers Association

Printed in the United States of America.
5 4 3 2 1

CONTENTS

INTRODUCTION

Ah, school days. . .or would that be school "daze"?

We've all been there, in one way or another. Whether public-schooled, home-schooled, or Sunday-schooled, we've all walked, run, or been dragged down those hallowed halls of learning. And we've all experienced the joys and trials of the educational process, which is what *The Teacher, Teacher Joke Book* is all about.

Readin', writin', and 'rithmetic? We've got you covered. Phys ed, fractions, and field trips? Got them, too. Whether you attend school now or you rode a dinosaur to the learning cave, you'll enjoy this erudite collection of funnies drawn from every aspect of education.

They say you should never stop learning. . .and, may we add, you should never stop *laughing,* either. If, as the Bible says, "a merry heart doeth good like a medicine," here's a powerful dose of humor to keep you healthy.

That's better than gym class, isn't it?

ANIMAL
ANTICS

What is gray and dusty and goes,
"Cough, cough"?
An elephant cleaning erasers.

Have you heard about the new magazine
in the library for athletic dogs?
It's called Spots Illustrated.

What kind of tests are fish good at?
Open brook tests.

A woman went to a pet store to buy a parrot. "I have three parrots," said the owner, "that were once owned by staff members of an elementary school. This one belonged to the principal."

"Squawk!" said the parrot. "You're expelled! You're expelled!"

The owner showed the woman the second parrot. "This one was kept by an English teacher."

"To be or not to be," said the parrot.

The woman was not interested in either one she had seen, so she asked to see the third parrot.

"This one belonged to the bus driver."

"And what does this parrot say?" she asked.

"Sit down and be quiet!" squawked the parrot. "Sit down and be quiet!"

Why was the sheep grounded?
He brought home a b-a-a-a-d report card.

Why did the pony have to go to the principal's office?
He was horsing around.

Why do spiders do so well in computer class?
They love the Web.

What fish does poorly in school?
Flounder.

Why did the lamb like its computer?
It was ewe-ser friendly.

Why did the giraffe graduate early?
He was head and shoulders above the rest.

✎ ✏

What is the first thing cows learn in school?
The alfalfa-bet.

✎ ✏

What is big and gray and goes, "Bubble, bubble, kaboom!"
An elephant experimenting with a chemistry set.

✎ ✏

What did the alligator say when he had a lot of homework to do?
"I'm swamped."

✎ ✏

What is the butterfly's favorite class?
Moth-ematics.

On the first day of school, the third-grade class found that their new teacher was a stallion. He was a large creature, but he had a high-pitched voice, and the class thought this was very funny. He spent most of his day yelling and screaming for order because the students didn't behave for him.

Finally, one day, the stallion lost his voice. He brought a pony into the class to help him out. The pony was small, but he had a deep, loud voice and demanded, "You kids pay attention or else you'll all be in trouble!"

The kids quickly quieted down and paid attention, which goes to show you: To get things done, you have to yell until you get a little horse.

What animal is best at math?
Rabbits, because they multiply fastest.

"MOST LIKELY TO SUCCEED":

Porcupines—they're sharp.

Fireflies—they're bright.

Rabbits—they're great at multiplying.

Hummingbirds—they finish their
hum-work.

Cats—they get purr-fect grades.

Elephants—they have lots of gray matter.

❧ ✑

"MOST LIKELY TO FAIL":

Squids—they can't ink straight.

Gorillas—they monkey around too much.

Mice—they just squeak by.

Cows—they copy off each udder.

Turtles—they're always late to class.

Lizards—they are always losing their
newt-books.

Squirrels—they drive the teacher nuts.

Parrots—they keep repeating their first
year.

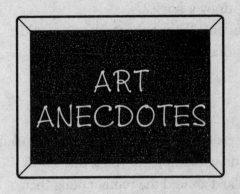

ART ANECDOTES

Art teacher to student: "What is your
   picture of?"
Student: "It's me when I accidentally hit
   my finger with a hammer."
Art teacher: "Oh, it's a self-portrait?"
Student: "No. It's a thumbnail sketch."

Art teacher: "I asked you to draw a cow
   eating some grass, but you've drawn
   only the cow."
Student: "The cow ate all the grass!"

Art teacher: "I asked that you draw a
    horse and wagon. Why did you only
    draw a horse?"
Student: "I thought the horse would
    draw the wagon."

A second-grade teacher asked her students
to draw examples of rings. She slowly
walked around the room, noting their
ideas. At Ed's desk, she stopped suddenly.

"Ed," she said, "those are all squares
and rectangles."

"No, they aren't," replied Ed. "They're
boxing rings."

Belle: "The art teacher doesn't like what
    I'm making."
Dad: "Why is that—what are you making?"
Belle: "Mistakes."

Yvonne's parents received a note from her second-grade teacher.

"Yvonne is a wonderful student," the teacher wrote, "but when we have art and coloring projects, she draws everything in dark blue. Grass, flowers, people, the sky, houses, cars, trees—everything is dark blue. This is unusual for a second-grade student. Might there be an explanation? If there is some sort of emotional problem, I would like to work with you to resolve it as quickly as possible."

That night, Yvonne's parents sat down with her and asked her why everything she drew was in dark blue. "Why is that such a special color to you?" they asked her.

"Well," she began slowly, "I didn't want to tell you, but a couple of weeks ago I lost my box of crayons. The only one I have left is the dark blue one I found in the bottom of my backpack."

CAFETERIA KIDDING

What is the worst thing you can find in the school cafeteria?

The food.

Did you hear about the cruel school cook?

She beats the eggs and whips the cream.

Student: "I thought we got a choice for
   lunch, but there's only hot dogs and
   fries."
Cafeteria worker: "Here's the choice—
   take it or leave it."

Student: "I don't like cheese with holes."
Cafeteria worker: "Well, just eat the
   cheese and throw the holes away."

Health teacher: "How many bones do
   you have in your body?"
Student: "Two thousand. I had fish for
   lunch in the cafeteria."

COLLEGE
COMEDY

A college student in his philosophy class was taking his first exam. On the paper there was one line, which read, "Is this a question? Discuss."

He thought for several minutes, then wrote, "If that is a question, then this is an answer."

He received an A on the exam.

Henry: "How did you pass the entrance
   exam for candy-making school?"
Greg: "It was simple. I fudged it."

Renee: "I took a course called 'How to
   Improve Your Concentration.'"
Kathryn: "Did you learn anything?"
Renee: "I'm sorry, did you just say
   something?"

During a Police Academy class, the
instructor began, "If you were called to
an automobile accident with the chief of
police in one car and the mayor in the
other car. . .then suddenly you looked
up to the top floor of a high-rise building across the street and saw a man
standing on the railing. . .then you
looked down the street and saw several

fire trucks were desperately fighting a fire in the courthouse. . .what would you do under these circumstances?"

One of the new recruits answered, "I'd remove my uniform and mingle with the crowd."

❧ ✎

Sue: "Did you like the decision-making course you took?"

Jill: "Yes and no."

❧ ✎

A college student delivered a pizza to the Wilsons' house. Mr. Wilson asked him, "What is the usual tip?"

"Well," he replied, "this is my first trip here, but the other guys say if I get a quarter out of you, I'll be doing great."

"Is that so?" snorted Mr. Wilson. "Well, just to show them how wrong they are, I'll give you five dollars."

"Thanks!" replied the delivery guy. "I'll put this toward my textbooks."

"What are you studying?" asked Mr. Wilson.

The young man smiled and said, "Psychology."

Students, take note:

Knowledge is power. . .
but power corrupts. . .
and corruption is a crime. . .
and crime doesn't pay. . .
so if you keep on studying,
   you'll go broke!

COURSE EVALUATION RESULTS

These are supposedly actual student comments taken from a college course evaluation:

"This class was a religious experience for me. I had to take it all on faith."

"Text makes a satisfying 'thud' when dropped on the floor."

"The class is worthwhile because I need it for the degree."

"His blackboard technique puts Rembrandt to shame."

"The textbook is confusing. Someone with a knowledge of English should proofread it."

"In class I learn I can fudge answers and get away with it."

"Keep lecturer or tenure board will be shot."

"The recitation instructor would make a

good parking lot attendant. Tries to tell you where to go, but you can never understand him."

"Text is useless. I use it to kill roaches in my room."

"I am convinced that you can learn by osmosis by just sitting in his class."

"Problem sets are a decoy to lure you away from potential exam material."

"Recitation was great. It was so confusing that I forgot who I was, where I was, and what I was doing—it's a great stress reliever."

"He is one of the best teachers I have had. He is well organized, presents good lectures, and creates interest in the subject. I hope my comments don't hurt his chances of getting tenure."

"I would sit in class and stare out the window at the squirrels. They've got a cool nest in the tree."

"He teaches like Speedy Gonzalez on a caffeine high."

"This course kept me out of trouble from 2:00–4:30 on Tuesdays and Thursdays."

"Information was presented like a ruptured fire hose—spraying in all directions—no way to stop it."

✎   ✏

It had been snowing for several hours when an announcement came over the campus intercom: "Will the students who are parked on University Drive please move their cars promptly? We must begin plowing."

Fifteen minutes later, there came

another announcement: "Will the nine hundred students who went to move thirty-four cars please return to class?"

What kind of tests are dental students good at?

True or floss.

A college junior was proudly showing off his new apartment to his friends. He led them into the living room.

"What are the big brass gong and hammer for?" one of his friends asked.

"That is my talking clock," he replied.

"How does it work?" his friend asked.

"I'll show you," the student said and proceeded to smash the gong with the hammer.

Suddenly, from the other side of the wall, a voice yelled, "Knock it off! It's 1:00 A.M.!"

Professor: "Are there any questions before you begin the final exam?"
Student: "What's the name of this course?"

A college freshman called his mom and asked her to send some money.

His mom said, "Sure, Son, I'll send some money. You also left your biology book when you visited a couple of weeks ago. Would you like me to send that, too?"

"Um. . .uh. . .yeah. . .okay," her son stammered.

So his mom packaged up the book and funds and went to the post office.

When she returned, her husband asked, "So, how much did you send him this time?"

"Well," she answered, "I wrote two checks—one for twenty dollars and the other for five hundred dollars."

"That's five hundred and twenty dollars!" exclaimed husband. "Are you crazy?"

"Don't worry, sweetheart," she said. "I taped the twenty-dollar check to the front of his biology book, but I put the five-hundred-dollar one somewhere between the pages of chapter eighteen!"

Optimist: A college student who opens his wallet and expects to find money.

Drew and Luis were late for their English Lit final exam. Thinking quickly, they rubbed some dirt and grease on their face and hands and agreed on an excuse. By the time they got to the room, the other students had already completed their exams and left.

"We're so sorry, Professor Morris," said Drew, "but on the way here, we got a flat tire, and Luis and I had to change it ourselves."

"Come back tomorrow," said Professor Morris, smiling. "I'll let you make it up then."

Drew and Luis were happy with the reprieve and spent the rest of the day playing outdoors.

The following morning, they arrived on time to complete the exam. The professor put the young men in separate rooms. The students found that there was only one question on the final exam. It read simply, "Which tire?"

Dear Mom and Dad,

Cla$$e$ are really great. I am making lot$ of friend$ and $tudying very hard. I $imply can't think of anything I need, $o if you would like, you can ju$t $end me a card, a$ I would love to hear from you. You're the be$t parent$!

Love, Your $on

The reply:

Dear Son,

We kNOw that astroNOmy, ecoNOmics, and oceaNOgraphy are eNOugh to keep even an hoNOr student busy. Do NOt forget that the pursuit of kNOwledge is a NOble task.

Will we see you in NOvember? We enjoyed getting your letter. Write aNOther one when you get some time.

Love, Mom and Dad

A college student was sitting in a philosophy class. His professor was debating the existence of God. He offered the following logic:

"Has anyone in this class heard God?"

No one responded.

"Has anyone in this class touched God?"

Again, no one answered.

"Has anyone in this class seen God?"

When no one replied, he simply stated, "Then there is no God."

The student disagreed with this announcement and asked for permission to speak. The professor granted it, and the student stood up and asked his classmates the following:

"Has anyone here heard our professor's brain?"

Silence.

"Has anyone here touched our professor's brain?"

Not a sound.

"Has anyone in this class seen our professor's brain?"

When no one in the class dared to speak, the student concluded, "Then, according to our professor's logic, it must be true that our professor does not have a brain!"

The student received an A in the class.

✐ ✐

FINAL EXAM

Instructions: Read each question carefully. Answer all questions.
Time limit: 4 hours. Begin immediately.

Art: Given one eight-count box of crayons and three sheets of notebook paper, recreate the ceiling of the Sistine Chapel. Skin tones should be true to life.

Chemistry: You must identify a poison sample, which you will find at your lab table. All necessary equipment has been provided. There are two beakers at your desk, one of which holds the antidote. If the wrong substance is used, it causes instant death. You may begin as soon as the professor injects you with a sample of the poison. (We feel this will give you incentive to find the correct answer.)

Civil Engineering: This is a practical test of your design and building skills. With the boxes of toothpicks and glue present, build a platform that will support your weight when you and your platform are suspended over a vat of nitric acid.

Computer Science: Write a fifth-generation computer language.

Using this language, write a computer program to finish the rest of this exam for you.

Economics: Develop a realistic plan for refinancing the national debt. Trace the possible effects of your plan in the following areas: Cubism, the Donatist Controversy, and the Wave Theory of Light. Outline a method from all possible points of view, as demonstrated in your answer to the last question.

Electrical Engineering: You will be placed in a nuclear reactor and given a partial copy of the electrical layout. The electrical system has been tampered with. You have seventeen minutes to find the problem and correct it before the reactor melts down.

Engineering: The disassembled parts of a

high-powered rifle have been placed on your desk. You will also find an instruction manual, printed in Swahili. In ten minutes, a hungry Bengal tiger will be let into the room. Take whatever action you feel appropriate. Be prepared to justify your decision.

Epistemology: Take a position for or against truth. Prove the validity of your stand.

General Knowledge: Describe in detail. Be objective and specific.

History: Describe the history of the papacy from its origin to the present day, concentrating especially, but not exclusively, on its social, political, economic, religious, and philosophical impact on Europe, Asia, America, and Africa. Be brief, concise, and specific.

Mathematics: Derive the Euler-Cauchy equations using only a straightedge and compass. Discuss in detail the role these equations had on mathematical analysis in Europe during the 1800s.

Philosophy: Sketch the development of human thought. Estimate its significance. Compare with the development of any other kind of thought.

Physics: Explain the nature of matter. Include in your answer an evaluation of the impact of the development of mathematics on science.

Political Science: There is a red telephone on the desk beside you. Start World War III. Report at length on its sociopolitical effects, if any.

Public Speaking: Twenty-five hundred

riot-crazed aborigines are storming the classroom. Calm them. You may use any ancient language except Latin or Greek.

Sociology: Estimate the sociological problems that might accompany the end of the world. Construct an experiment to test your theory.

Extra Credit: Define the universe and give three examples.

If you finish early, turn your paper in at the table at the front of the room.

Benjamin had studied all night for his calculus final, but when it came time for the exam, he felt that he still was not ready.

The professor distributed the exams

and told the class that they had sixty minutes to complete it. Every five minutes, he reminded the class how much time was left. This made Benjamin only more anxious and frustrated.

Finally, after sixty minutes, the professor announced, "The exam is over. Turn them in!"

One by one, the papers were handed in, but Benjamin kept working on his exam. The professor decided to wait and see how long it would take him.

After another twenty minutes, Benjamin walked to the professor's desk to hand in his exam. The professor asked him, "What are you doing?"

Benjamin answered, "I'm turning in my exam."

The professor replied, "The exam was over twenty minutes ago. You have failed!"

Benjamin looked the professor in the eye and asked, "Do you know who I am?"

The professor answered, "No, I don't

know who you are."

Benjamin asked, "Are you sure you don't know who I am?"

"No!" said the professor, becoming rather annoyed. "And that really doesn't matter."

Benjamin then picked up half of the stack of completed exams, placed his in the stack, and put the others back on top. "Good!" he exclaimed and ran out of the room.

✎ ✏

A professor was giving a test to his students. He handed out the tests and then sat down at his desk to wait. Soon, the test was over, and the students all handed the tests back in.

The professor looked through the completed exams and noticed one of his students had attached a one-hundred-dollar bill to his test with a note reading,

"A dollar per point."

The next class, the professor handed back the graded tests. The student got his test back with fifty-three dollars in change.

❧   ✎

A college freshman returned to his dorm room and found that his mother had come for a surprise visit. She wanted to find out how he was doing, adjusting to college life.

"How do you get along with the other students?" she asked.

"Mom," he replied, "all the guys on this hall are so loud. The one on that side keeps banging something on the wall and won't stop. The one on the other side screams and screams all night."

"Oh dear!" his mother said. "How can you put up with such noisy neighbors?".

"Well," he answered, "I just ignore them and keep playing my drums."

FUN THINGS TO DO ON A FINAL THAT DOES NOT MATTER:

- Bring a pillow. Fall asleep (or pretend to) until the last fifteen minutes. Wake up, say, "Oh no, I'd better get started!" and do some gibberish work. Turn it in early.

- Get a copy of the exam, then run out screaming, "Andre, Andre, I've got the secret documents!"

- If it's a math test, answer in essay form.

- If it's an essay test, answer with numbers and symbols. Be creative.

- Make paper airplanes out of the exam. Aim them at the instructor's nose.

- Talk throughout the exam. Read questions aloud. Debate your answers with yourself out loud.

- Bring cheerleaders.

- Walk in, get the exam, and sit down. About three minutes into it, look at the instructor and say, "I don't understand *any* of this. I've been to every class! What's the deal? And who are you? Where's the regular guy?"

- Bring a Game Boy (or Game Gear, etc.). Play it with the volume at max level.

- Bring pets.

- Fifteen minutes into the exam, stand up, rip your exam into very small pieces, throw them into the air, and yell out, "Merry Christmas!" If you're really daring, ask for another copy of the exam. Say you lost the first one. Repeat this process every fifteen minutes.

- Do the exam with crayons, paint, or fluorescent markers.

- Come into the exam wearing slippers, a bathrobe, and a towel on your head.

- Do the entire exam in another language. If you don't know one, make one up. For math and science exams, try using Roman numerals.

- As soon as the instructor hands you the exam, eat it.

- Every five minutes, stand up, collect all your things, move to another seat, and continue with the exam.

- Turn in the exam approximately fifteen minutes into it. As you walk out, comment on how easy it was.

- Do the entire exam as if it were multiple choice and true/false. If it is a multiple-choice exam, spell out words with your answers (CAB, BAD, BABE, etc.).

- Bring a black marker. Return the exam with all questions and answers completely blacked out.

- Bring a water pistol with you. Enough said.

- From the moment the exam begins, hum the theme to *Jeopardy*.

- If the exam is math or science related, make up the longest proofs you can possibly think of. Get *pi* and

imaginary numbers into most equations. If it is a written exam, relate everything to your own life story.

* Come in wearing a full knight's outfit, complete with sword and shield.

* Bring a friend to give you a back massage during the exam. Convince the instructor that this person is needed because you have poor circulation.

* After you get the exam, call the instructor over, point to any question, and ask for the answer. Try to work it out of him/her.

* Bring balloons and/or beach balls, blow them up, and start throwing them around the room.

* Try to get people in the room to do the wave.

- Play Frisbee with a friend on the other side of the room.

- Get deliveries of candy, flowers, balloons, food, or telegrams sent to you every few minutes during the exam.

- During the exam, take apart everything around you—desks, chairs, anything you can reach.

- Bring a musical instrument with you. Play various tunes. If you are asked to stop, explain, "It helps me think." Bring a copy of the student handbook with you, challenging the instructor to find the section on musical instruments during finals.

✎ ✐

Rick is working toward a degree in physical science. Each day he asks,

"Why does this work?"

Penny is working toward a degree in mechanical engineering. Each day she asks, "How does this work?"

Ty is working toward a degree in economics. Each day he asks, "How much does it cost to manufacture this?"

Christine is working toward a degree in chemistry. Each day she asks, "Could this be hazardous to the environment?"

Phil is working toward a degree in liberal arts. Each day he asks, "Would you like fries with that?"

"What was the principal occupation of the ancient Babylonians?" the history professor asked.

"Dying, I believe," answered a student.

A linguistics professor was lecturing his class one day. "In the English language," he said, "a double negative forms a positive. In other languages, such as Russian, a double negative is still a negative. However, there is no language wherein a double positive can form a negative."

A voice from the back of the room said, "Yeah, right."

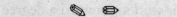

THE ART OF GRADING

This is how various professors grade their final exams:

Department of Statistics:
   All grades are plotted along the normal bell curve.

Department of Psychology:
   Students are asked to blot ink in their

exam books, close them, and turn them in. The professor opens the books and assigns the first grade that comes to mind.

Department of History:
All students get the same grade they got last year.

Department of Philosophy:
What is a grade?

School of Law:
Students are asked to defend their position of why they should receive an A.

Department of Mathematics:
Grades are variable.

Department of Logic:
If and only if the student is present for the final and the student has

accumulated a passing grade, then the
student will receive an A, else the
student will not receive an A.

Department of Computer Science:
Random number generator deter-
mines grade.

Department of Music:
Each student must figure out his
grade by listening to the instructor
play the corresponding note (+ and -
would be sharp and flat, respectively).

✎ ✐

SIGNS YOU'RE SUFFERING FROM SEMESTER BURNOUT:

Your parents inquire about your grades,
and you break into singing the Cookie
Monster song: "C is for cookie; that's
good enough for me. . . ."

You wake up to discover your bed is on fire, but you go back to sleep because you really don't care.

Just to get a break from studying, you actually exit your dormitory when the nightly fire alarm goes off.

You sleep more in class than in your bed.

Thoughts of the upcoming weekend help you make it through Monday.

The McDonald's workers know your name and what you usually order as a result of those late-night study breaks.

You have spent more time calculating that you need only a 62% on the final to pass the class than actual time studying for the final.

The test papers are no longer worthy of the fridge door.

Your absence exceeds your attendance.

THINGS I LEARNED IN COLLEGE:

That it didn't matter how late I scheduled my first class—I'd still sleep through it.

That I could change so much and barely realize it.

That college kids throw airplanes, too.

That if you wear polyester, everyone will ask, "Why are you so dressed up?"

That every clock on campus shows a different time.

That if you were smart in high school—
so what?

That chemistry labs require more time
than all my classes put together.

That you can know everything and fail
a test.

That you can know nothing and ace
a test.

That most of my education would be
obtained outside of my classes.

That I would be one of those people my
parents warned me about.

That free food served until 10:00 is gone
by 9:50.

That psychology is really biology, and
that biology is really chemistry, that

chemistry is really physics, and physics is really math.

FIVE RANDOM TIPS
FOR SURVIVING COLLEGE:

1) Enjoy being a sophomore—it could be the best three years of your life.

2) If an 8:00 A.M. class is required for your major, change your major.

3) If you're sitting through a boring lecture, start a wave!

4) College-level math: 5 returnable bottles = 1 delicious Ramen Noodle dinner.

5) Clever margin manipulation can turn a three-page outline into a fifty-page essay.

You Might Be a College Student. . .

If you have ever price-shopped for Top Ramen.

If you live in a house with three couches, none of which match.

If you consider "mac and cheese" a balanced meal.

If you have ever written a check for forty-five cents.

If you have ever seen two consecutive sunrises without sleeping.

If your glass set is composed of McDonald's Extra Value Meal plastic cups.

If you cannot remember when you last washed your car.

If you can pack your worldly possessions into the back of a pickup (in one trip).

If you average less than three hours of sleep a night.

If your trash is overflowing and your bank account isn't.

If you go to Wal-Mart more than three times a week.

If you eat at the cafeteria because it's "free," even though it tastes terrible.

If you are personally keeping the local pizza place from bankruptcy.

If you wake up ten minutes before class.

If you wear the same jeans nine days in a row—without washing them.

If your breakfast consists of a Coke on the way to class.

If your social life consists of a date with the library.

If your idea of "doing your hair" is putting on a baseball cap.

If it takes a shovel to find the floor of your room.

If you carry less than a dollar on you at all times because that's all you have.

If you haven't done laundry in so long you are wearing your swimsuit to class.

If your midnight snack is microwave popcorn.

If you celebrate when you find a quarter.

If you wear a sweat suit for so long that it stands up by itself.

If your backpack is giving you scoliosis.

If you can sleep through your roommate's blaring stereo.

If you live in an area that is smaller than most mobile homes.

If you get more E-mail than "snail" mail.

College would be great if it weren't for all the classes.

A speaker was scheduled to address an audience at a university. A couple of hours before she was to take the podium, some student pranksters took all of the folding chairs, loaded them into their vehicles, and drove away. No one was aware of the problem until the audience began arriving for the lecture. There wasn't enough time to find more chairs, so everyone had to stand while she spoke.

That evening, she decided to write to her mother to let her know how the speech went. "It was a huge success," she wrote. "Hours before I arrived, every seat in the house was taken, and I was given a standing ovation throughout my speech."

What did the meteorology student say about his final exam?

"It was a breeze with only a few foggy patches."

A man was visiting a college. He paused to admire the new Hemingway Hall that had recently been constructed on campus.

"It's marvelous to see a building named for Ernest Hemingway," he said.

"Actually," said the guide, "it's named for William Hemingway. No relation."

The visitor was astonished. "Was William Hemingway a writer, too?" he asked.

"Oh, yes," said his guide. "He wrote the check."

✎   ✏

A professor was discussing a particularly complicated concept. A premed student rudely interrupted him and asked, "Why do we have to learn this pointless information?"

"To save lives," the professor responded quickly and continued the lecture.

A few minutes later, the same student

spoke up again. "So how does physics save lives?" he inquired.

"It keeps people like you out of medical school," replied the professor.

A college professor noticed that one of his students was habitually late to class. Before class ended for the day, he went around the room asking students some questions about that day's lecture. Of course, he made sure to pick on the tardy student.

"And who was it that developed the theories behind Communism?" the professor asked.

"I don't know," came the reply.

"Perhaps if you came to class on time, you would know," said the professor.

"That's not true," the student replied. "I can never pay attention anyway!"

A student studied very hard for a course on birds. On the day of the final, he was stunned when the teacher told the students that their task was to identify twenty birds by viewing pictures of only their legs.

Although the student had prepared well for the exam, he hadn't studied anything about legs. He was frustrated and got up to leave. "Just a moment," the instructor said, "what is your name?"

The student pulled up his pant legs and said, "Guess!"

A college student remembered his father's birthday was just days away. He sent a cheap present with a note reading, "Dear Dad, I know this isn't much, but it is all you can afford."

A professor asked a student to stay for a moment after class.

Holding the young man's assignment, the professor asked, "Did you write this poem by yourself?"

The student said, "Yes, I did—every word of it."

The professor extended his hand and said, "Well, then, I'm very glad to meet you, Mr. Wordsworth. I thought you had been dead for quite some time!"

An English professor wrote the following words on the blackboard: "Woman without her man is nothing." He then requested that his students punctuate it correctly.

The men wrote: "Woman, without her man, is nothing."

The women wrote: "Woman! Without her, man is nothing."

COMPUTER CRAZINESS

What kind of computer would you find
in the Garden of Eden?

Adam's Apple.

What did the computer programmer say
to the waiter?

"May I see a pull-down menu, please?"

Why did the computer go to the doctor?
It caught a bug.

Why shouldn't computers drive cars?
Because they're always crashing.

A computer technician was called to the school to repair a computer. He wasn't able to find a close parking spot, so he left his car in a no-parking zone and placed a note on his windshield saying, "Scott Brown, computer technician, working inside the building."

He was finished working within an hour, and when he returned to his car, he found a ticket with a note that read, "David Jackson, police officer, working outside the building."

DISCIPLINE DROLLERY

A teacher called the mother of one of her students. "I have bad news and good news about Dan. The bad news is he is the worst-behaved student in my class."

"Well, what's the good news?" asked Dan's mother.

"The good news is that he has perfect attendance."

Mom: "If you passed the test, why did your teacher fail you?"

Brad: "Because I passed it to Nate."

One afternoon, Carl was sent to the principal's office. "Do you know why you're here?" asked the principal.

"Is it about this morning?" Carl asked.

"Your teacher says that you disrupted class, hit another student, started a food fight at lunchtime, and ran in the hall."

"Oh, that's a relief," said Carl. "I thought maybe you figured out I was the one who broke your windshield."

Each week, Ricky was sent to the principal's office for some kind of trouble. One day, about halfway through the school year, the principal said, "Ricky, I'm really getting tired of seeing you here, week after week. What do you think I should do about it?"

"Well," said Ricky, "if you really don't like it here, maybe you should get transferred to another school."

✏️ ✏️

Dad: "Why were you expelled from school?"

Matt: "I used a hose to fill up the swimming pool."

Dad: "I didn't know the school had a swimming pool."

Matt: "Well, it does now!"

✏️ ✏️

Teacher: "This is the third time I've had to send you to the principal's office this week. What do you have to say for yourself?"

Student: "Thank goodness it's Friday!"

Dad: "How do you stand in school, Ted?"
Ted: "Usually in the corner."

A student was told to go to the back of the line for being too rowdy while waiting to enter the cafeteria. Within a minute, the teacher found him again at the front of the line.

"What are you doing?" asked the teacher. "I sent you to the back of the line."

"Well, I went, but there's already somebody back there."

An unruly student was sent to the principal's office.
Principal: "Do you ever complete your homework?"
Student: "Oh, every now and then."
Principal: "Where do you do it?"

Student: "Oh, here and there."
Principal: "You're going to detention!"
Student: "When will I get out?"
Principal: "Oh, sooner or later."

Teacher: "Mrs. Baker, I've asked you to
   come in today to discuss Brooke's
   appearance."
Mrs. Baker: "Why? What is wrong with
   her appearance?"
Teacher: "She hasn't made one in my
   classroom since September!"

The best part of going back to school is
seeing all your friends. The worst part is
that your teachers won't let you talk to
them.

On the first day of class, the teacher asked if anyone was planning on causing trouble in her class. "If so," she said, "please stand up." After a few moments of silence, a little girl stood up. "Are you going to cause trouble?" the teacher asked.

"Oh, no," replied the girl. "I just didn't want you to have to stand there all by yourself."

A frustrated father vented, "When I was a teenager and got in trouble, I was sent to my room without supper. But my son has his own color TV, telephone, computer, and CD player in his room."

"So what do you do to him?" asked his friend.

"I send him to *my* room!" exclaimed the father.

Playing hooky is like a credit card—fun now, pay later.

Teacher: "I would like to go through one whole day without having to tell you to behave."
Student: "You have my permission."

Laugh, and the class laughs with you—but you get detention alone.

Teacher: "Would you two at the back of the room stop passing notes?"
Student: "We're not passing notes. We're playing cards."

FIELD TRIP
FUNNIES

Teacher: "Class, are you looking forward
to our field trip to the national tree
museum?"
Student: "Well, I could take it or leaf it."

A third-grade class went to an art
museum. They were instructed to sit
and wait until the guide was ready to
begin the tour. Two boys, however,
decided to explore on their own.

They walked down a hallway and entered a room filled with modern art pieces.

"Quick," said one. "Run—before they say *we* did it!"

Mom: "Julie, why aren't you going on the field trip to the Mint?"
Julie: "It just doesn't make a lot of cents to me."

A first-grade class went on a field trip to the local police station. An officer was showing them around and stopped in front of a "Ten Most Wanted" poster. He explained how citizens often help bring about their arrests.

"Are those pictures of the bad guys?" a child asked.

"Yes, those are the bad guys," the policeman answered.

"Well," said the child, "why didn't you hold on to them when you took their pictures?"

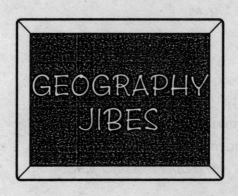

GEOGRAPHY JIBES

Teacher: "Please name two ranges."
Student: "Gas and electric."

Teacher: "Fred, can you find Australia on the map for me, please?"
Fred: "There it is."
Teacher: "Now, Louise, who discovered Australia?"
Louise: "Fred did!"

What is the most slippery country in the world?

Greece.

What's the difference between an American student and an English student?

About three thousand miles.

Why is Alabama the smartest state in the U.S.A.?

It has four As and a B.

"It's obvious," said the teacher, "that you haven't studied your geography. What is your excuse?"

"Well," the student replied, "my dad

says the world is changing every day, so I thought it would be best if I waited until it settles down."

❧　✐

Teacher: "What are the small rivers that run into the Nile?"
Student: "The juve-Niles."

❧　✐

Teacher: "Why is the Mississippi such an unusual river?"
Student: "Because it has four *I*s and can't see."

❧　✐

Teacher: "What are the Great Plains?"
Student: "The 747, Concorde, and F-16."

Teacher: "Where is the English Channel?"
Student: "I don't know; we don't get that
    one on our TV."

GRADING GIGGLES

Immanuel: "Do you think anyone can really tell the future with cards?"

Taylor: "My mom can. She took a look at my report card and told me exactly what was going to happen when my dad got home."

Shortly after Christmas vacation, Eddy came home with a bad report card. His mother asked him, "What was the trouble?"

Eddy answered, "Oh, there was no trouble. Thing are always marked down after the holidays."

Mother: "This is the worst report card I have ever seen! What do you have to say for yourself?"

Ned: "Well, at least you know I'm not cheating!"

Jen: "Dad, I got a 100 in school today!"

Dad: "That's great! What did you get it in?"

Jen: "Two subjects: a 40 in math and a 60 in history."

Father: "How are your grades, Peter?"
Peter: "They're underwater, Dad."
Father: "What do you mean, under-
    water?"
Peter: "They're below C level."

A third-grade boy walked up to his
teacher's desk, holding a report card with
a big red F. "If I were you," said Peter,
"I would change this right away."

"Why is that?" asked the teacher.

"Because my daddy told me that if
I brought home one more failing report
card, someone was going to get in big
trouble!"

A mother and father were paying bills
one evening.

"Groceries, gasoline, electricity—

everything is going up," mused the father.

"I know," agreed the mother. "Nothing ever goes down."

"Well, look at this!" exclaimed their son, walking into the room with his report card.

The father of a high-school student called the geometry teacher and demanded to know why his son had received an F on his midterm exam.

"Because I can't give a G," answered the teacher.

Mother: "Why does your test have a big zero at the top of it?"
Son: "That's not a zero. The teacher ran out of stars, so she gave me a moon instead."

Shelly: "I failed every subject except for
    algebra."
Leanne: "How did you keep from failing
    that?"
Shelly: "I didn't take algebra."

Maria stood quietly as her father exam-
ined her report card.

"What is this 45 in math?" her father
asked.

"I think that's the number of people
in the class," she answered quickly.

Father: "You have four Ds and a C on
    your report card!"
Son: "Maybe I concentrated too much on
    the one subject."

A tenth-grade boy came home with a poor report card. As he handed it to his father, he asked, "What do you think is wrong, Dad, my heredity or my environment?"

Mother: "Does your teacher like you?"
Son: "Like me? She loves me! Look at all those Xs on my test."

"Will, I think the reason you're getting such bad grades is because you spend too much time watching game shows on TV."

"Dad, could you please phrase that in the form of a question?"

Teacher: "Felix, when is the boiling point reached?"

Felix: "Just after my father reads my report card."

HISTORY
HUMOR

Teacher: "We are going to watch a video
about the history of medicine."
Student: "Oh, no, not another
doc-umentary!"

Where in the U.S. Constitution does it
say that it's okay to wear sleeveless shirts?
The part that says, "The right to bear
arms."

Teacher: "What is your report on?"
James: "The history of underwear."
Teacher: "Will it be long?"
James: "No, it will be brief."

"What do you think was the most important invention in all of history?" the teacher asked her class.

"The automobile," answered one student.

"The airplane," answered the second.

"The nuclear submarine," answered the third.

"The credit card," answered the fourth.

What is the fruitiest lesson?
History, because it's full of dates.

Dad: "How could you flunk history?"

Deb: "Because everything my teacher says goes in both ears and out the other."

Dad: "But that's three ears!"

Deb: "I'm not doing very well in math, either."

Teacher: "How was the Roman Empire cut in half?"

Student: "With a pair of Caesars."

Teacher: "In 1940, what were the Poles doing in Russia?"

Student: "Holding up the telegraph lines."

Jake: "I wish we lived in the olden days."

Teacher: "Why is that?"

Jake: "We wouldn't have so much history
   to learn!"

Teacher: "Please tell me something
   important that didn't exist fifty
   years ago."
Natalie: "Me!"

Teacher: "Zach, you need to work on
   learning the presidents. When I was
   your age, I could name all of them."
Zach: "Yes, but then there were only four
   or five."

Teacher: "Where was the Declaration of
   Independence signed?"
Vicki: "At the bottom."

Teacher: "What happened in 1809?"
Jody: "Abraham Lincoln was born."
Teacher: "Right. Now, what happened
    in 1812?"
Jody: "He turned three years old."

What bus crossed the ocean?
    Columbus.

History teacher: "Why was George
    Washington standing in the bow of
    the boat as the army crossed the
    Delaware?"
Student: "Because he knew if he sat
    down, he would have to row."

WORLD HISTORY

The following is a "history" collected by teachers throughout the United States, from students in the eighth grade through college level.

The inhabitants of ancient Egypt were called mummies. They lived in the Sarah Dessert and traveled by Camelot. The climate of the Sarah is such that the inhabitants have to live elsewhere, so areas of the dessert are cultivated by irritation. The Egyptians built the Pyramids in the shape of a huge triangular cube. The Pyramids are a range of mountains between France and Spain.

The Bible is full of interesting caricatures. In the first book of the Bible, Guinesses, Adam and Eve were created from an apple tree. One of their children, Cain, once asked, "Am I my brother's son?"

God asked Abraham to sacrifice Isaac on Mount Montezuma.

Jacob, son of Isaac, stole his brother's birthmark. Jacob was a patriarch who brought up his twelve sons to be patriarchs, but they did not take it. One of Jacob's sons, Joseph, gave refuse to the Israelites.

Pharaoh forced the Hebrew slaves to make bread without straw. Moses led them to the Red Sea, where they made unleavened bread, which is bread made without any ingredients. Afterwards, Moses went up on Mount Cyanide to get the Ten Commandments.

David was a Hebrew king skilled at playing the liar. He fought with the Philatelists, a race of people who lived in the Biblical times. Solomon, one of David's sons, had 500 wives and 500 porcupines.

Without the Greeks, we wouldn't have history. The Greeks invented three kinds of columns—Corinthian, Doric, and Ironic. They also had myths. A myth is a female moth. One myth says that the mother of Achilles dipped him in the River Stynx until he became intolerable. Achilles appears in *The Iliad*, by Homer. Homer also wrote *The Oddity*, in which Penelope was the last hardship that Ulysses endured on his journey. Actually, Homer was not written by Homer but by another man of that name.

Socrates was a famous Greek teacher who went around giving people advice. They killed him. Socrates died from an overdose of wedlock.

In the Olympic games, Greeks ran races, jumped, hurled the biscuits, and threw the java. The reward to the victor was a coral wreath.

The government of Athens was demo-
cratic because people took the law into
their own hands. There were no wars in
Greece, as the mountains were so high
that they couldn't climb over to see what
their neighbors were doing. When they
fought with the Persians, the Greeks
were outnumbered because the Persians
had more men.

Eventually, the Romans conquered the
Greeks. History calls people Romans
because they never stayed in one place
for very long. At Roman banquets, the
guests wore garlic in their hair. Julius
Caesar extinguished himself on the
battlefields of Gaul. The Ides of March
murdered him because they thought he
was going to be made king.

Nero was a cruel tyranny who would
torture his poor subjects by playing the
fiddle to them.

Then came the Middle Ages. King Alfred conquered the Dames. King Arthur lived in the Age of Shivery; King Harold mustarded his troops before the Battle of Hastings; and Joan of Arc was canonized by Bernard Shaw.

The Magna Carta provided that no free man should be hanged twice for the same offense.

In medieval times, most of the people were alliterate. The greatest writer of the time was Chaucer, who wrote many poems and versus and also wrote literature. Another tale tells of William Tell, who shot an arrow through an apple while standing on his son's head.

The Renaissance was an age in which more individuals felt the value of their human being. It was an age of great inventions and discoveries. Gutenberg invented the Bible. Another important invention was the circulation of blood.

The government of England was a limited mockery. Henry VIII found walking difficult because he had an abbess on his knee. Queen Elizabeth was a success. Her navy went out and defeated the Spanish Armadillo.

The greatest writer of the Renaissance was William Shakespeare. Shakespeare never made much money and is only famous because of his plays. He lived at Windsor with his merry wives, writing tragedies, comedies, and errors. In one of Shakespeare's famous plays, Lady MacBeth tried to convince MacBeth to kill the king. Romeo and Juliet are an example of a heroic couplet.

Writing at the same time as Shakespeare was Miguel Cervantes. He wrote *Donkey Hote*. The next great author was John Milton. Milton wrote *Paradise Lost*. Then his wife died and he wrote *Paradise Regained*.

During the Renaissance, America began. Christopher Columbus was a great navigator who discovered America. His ships were called the Nina, the Pinta, and the Santa Fe. Later, the Pilgrims crossed the ocean, and this was known as Pilgrims Progress. When they landed at Plymouth Rock, they were greeted by the Indians, who came down the hill rolling their war hoops before them. The Indian squabs carried porpoises on their backs. Many of the Indian heroes were killed, along with their cabooses, which proved very fatal for them. The winter of 1620 was a hard one for the settlers. Many people died and many babies were born. Captain

John Smith was responsible for all this.

One of the causes of the Revolutionary War was the English put tacks in their tea. Also, the colonists would send their parcels through the post without stamps. During the War, the Red Coats and Paul Revere were throwing balls over stone walls. The dogs were barking and the peacocks crowing. Finally, the colonists won the war and no longer had to pay for taxis.

Delegates from the original thirteen states formed the Contented Congress. Thomas Jefferson, a Virgin, and Benjamin Franklin were two singers of the Declaration of Independence.

Franklin had gone to Boston carrying all his clothes in his pocket and a loaf of bread under each arm. He invented electricity by rubbing two cats backwards and declared, "A horse divided against itself cannot stand." Franklin died in 1790 and is still dead.

George Washington married Martha Curtis and in due time became the Father of Our Country. Then the Constitution of the United States was adopted to secure domestic hostility. Under the Constitution, the people enjoyed the right to keep bare arms.

Abraham Lincoln became America's greatest president. Lincoln's mother died in infancy, and he was born in a log cabin which he built with his own hands. When Lincoln was president, he wore only a tall silk hat. He said, "In onion there is strength." Abraham Lincoln wrote the Gettysburg Address while traveling from Washington to Gettysburg on the back of an envelope. He also freed the slaves by signing the Emasculation Proclamation.

On the night of April 14, 1865, Lincoln went to the theater and got shot in his seat by one of the actors in a moving picture show. The believed assassinator was John Wilkes Booth, a supposedly insane actor. This ruined Booth's career. Meanwhile in Europe, the Enlightenment was a reasonable time. Voltare invented electricity and also wrote a book called *Candy*. Gravity was invented by Isaac Walton. It is chiefly noticeable in the autumn, when the apples are falling off trees.

Bach was the most famous composer in the world, and so was Handel. Handel was half German, half Italian, and half English. He was very large. Bach died from 1750 to the present. Beethoven wrote music even though he was deaf. He was so deaf he wrote loud music. He took long walks in the forest even when everyone was calling for him. Beethoven expired in 1827 and later died for this.

France was in a very serious state. The French Revolution was accomplished before it happened. The "Marseillaise" was the theme song of the French Revolution, and it catapulted into Napoleon.

During the Napoleonic Wars, the crowned heads of Europe were trembling in their shoes. The Spanish gorillas came down from the hills and nipped at Napoleon's flanks. He wanted an heir to inherit his power, but since Josephine was a baroness, she couldn't bear children.

Queen Victoria was the longest queen. She sat on a thorn for sixty-three years. Her reclining years and finally the end of her life were exemplary of a great personality. Her death was the final event which ended her reign.

The sun never set on the British Empire because the British Empire is in the east and the sun sets in the west.

The nineteenth century was a time of many great inventions and thoughts. The invention of the steamboat caused a network of rivers to spring up. Samuel Morse invented a code of telepathy. Louis Pasteur discovered a cure for rabbis. Charles Darwin was a naturalist who wrote the *Organ of the Species*.

History teacher: "Brad, what happened in 1492?"
Brad: "I don't know. I wasn't alive back then."

What's a history teacher's favorite quiz show?

The Dating Game.

✎ ✏

Teacher: "What was the greatest accomplishment of the early Romans?"
Student: "Speaking Latin."

✎ ✏

History teacher: "Who succeeded the first president of the U.S.A?"
Student: "The second one."

✎ ✏

Teacher: "What was Camelot?"
Student: "A place where people parked their camels."

Teacher: "What was Camelot famous
      for?"
Student: "Its knight life."

History teacher: "What was the first
      thing Queen Elizabeth did upon
      ascending the throne?"
Student: "She sat down."

"My teacher reminds me of history. She's
always repeating herself."

What do history teachers make when
they want to get together?
      Dates.

What do history teachers like to talk about?
The good old days.

Teacher: "Why did the pioneers cross the
country in covered wagons?"
Student: "Because they didn't want to
wait forty years for a train."

Teacher: "Why are you reading the last
pages of your history book first?"
Student: "I want to know how it ends."

A seventh-grade student was having dif-
ficulty completing his homework. Finally,
he slammed his textbook shut, threw down
his pencil, and informed his parents, "I've
decided I'm a conscientious objector."

"Why did you decide that?" asked his father.

"Because wars create too much history."

History teacher: "Who was the most famous Egyptian in history?"
Student: "The Mummy."

"What did Paul Revere say at the end of his famous ride?" quizzed the teacher.

A student answered, "Whoa!"

"Can anyone name the Roman emperor who was most notorious for persecuting early Christians?" asked the history teacher.

"Nero," answered a student.

"That's right. What were some of the things he did?"

"He tortured the prisoners in Rome."

"And do you know how he tortured them?"

"He played the fiddle."

HOMEWORK HILARITY

Teacher: "I just don't understand how one person can make this many mistakes on her homework!"

Ellen: "It wasn't one person. My dad helped me."

Rex: "Teacher, will I get in trouble for something I didn't do?"

Teacher: "No, Rex. Why?"

Rex: "Because I didn't do my homework."

Sheila: "The dog ate my homework!"
Teacher: "Sheila, do you have a dog?"
Sheila: "Well, no, it was a stray."

The following is an explanation of the school homework policy for the average student: "Students should not spend more than ninety minutes per night on an assignment. This time should be budgeted in the following manner if the student desires to achieve moderate to good grades in his/her classes."

Eleven minutes looking for the assignment.

Fourteen minutes calling a friend for the assignment.

Seventeen minutes explaining why the teacher is so unfair.

Nine minutes in the bathroom.

Twelve minutes getting a snack.

Eight minutes checking the *TV Guide*.

Nine minutes telling parents that the teacher never explained the assignment.

Ten minutes sitting at the kitchen table waiting for Mom or Dad to do the assignment.

Student: "I didn't do my homework because I lost my memory."
Teacher: "When did this start?"
Student: "When did what start?"

Son: "Dad, I'm tired of doing homework."
Father: "Hard work never killed anyone, you know."

Son: "I know. But I don't want to be the first!"

A mother was scolding her son for his habit of procrastinating when it came time for homework. "You really need to change," she encouraged.

"I know, Mom," he agreed. "I'll start on Monday."

Son: "Dad, will you help me with my homework?"
Father: "I'm sorry, Son. It wouldn't be right."
Son: "Well, at least you could try, couldn't you?"

HOMEWORK EXCUSES:

"I was on a ship, and it sprung a leak. I plugged the hole with my homework and saved hundreds of lives."

"I left it in my shirt, and my mother put it into the washing machine."

"My sister used it to line the rabbit's cage."

"I put it in a safe, but I lost the combination."

"A sudden gust of wind blew it out of my hand, and I never saw it again."

"I loaned it to a friend, but she suddenly moved away."

"My friend fell into a lake, and I jumped in to rescue him. My homework didn't make it, though."

"I lost it fighting this kid who said you *weren't* the best teacher in the whole world."

"Why is the paper blank? Well, because I used invisible ink!"

"Our furnace stopped working, and we had to burn it to keep ourselves from freezing."

"I didn't do it because I didn't want the other kids in the class to look bad."

"I know the importance of recycling, so I did my part by recycling it."

"I did my report on the history of pizza. It was so good that my little sister ate it."

"The lights in our house went out, and I had to burn it to get enough light to see the fuse box."

"My uncle built a time machine and took my homework with him. You should have received it about two years ago."

"I didn't do it because I didn't want to add to your already heavy workload."

JANITOR
JOKES

A middle school was faced with a problem. After putting on their lipstick, some girls would pucker up and press their lips against the bathroom mirrors, leaving many lip prints.

One day, the principal thought of a way to put an end to this problem. She called all the girls to the bathroom and had the custodian meet them there. She explained to the girls that the lip prints were causing extra work for the custodian because he had to clean the mirrors every day.

To prove to the girls how difficult it was for him to clean the mirrors, she asked the custodian to clean one of the mirrors. He took out a long-handled brush, dipped it into the nearest toilet, and thoroughly scrubbed the mirror. No lip prints were seen on the mirrors again.

Why did the custodian quit his job?
He wanted to make a clean sweep.

LIBRARY LAUGHS

How do librarians catch fish?
With bookworms.

Student: "I'd like to check out this book on blood clots."
Librarian: "I'm sorry, that doesn't circulate."

Have you heard about the baker who wrote a mystery novel?

It's a real who-donut.

Why was the library so tall?

Because it had so many stories.

Did you hear about the delivery van loaded with thesauruses that crashed into a bus?

Witnesses were shocked, astounded, surprised, taken aback, dumbfounded, thunderstruck, startled, caught unaware. . . .

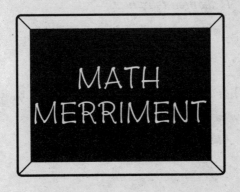

MATH
MERRIMENT

Teacher: "Define 'absolute zero.'"
Greg: "The lowest grade you can get on a test."

Teacher: "What is one-sixtieth of an hour, or sixty seconds?"
Heidi: "Give me a minute, and I'll remember."

Why did the fraction want to go on a diet?

It wanted to reduce.

What do math teachers take when they have a cold?

Alka-Seltzer Plus.

What do math teachers like to eat with their coffee?

A slice of pi.

What numbers are always wandering around?

Roamin' numerals.

Teacher: "If you ran 876 yards on Monday
and ran the same distance again on
Tuesday, what would you get?"

Al: "Exhausted!"

"Knock-knock!"
  "Who's there?"
"Imus."
  "Imus who?"
"Imus get an A on my math test!"

Dad: "Did you pass algebra?"

Sam: "I sure did!"

Dad: "Then why does your report
card show an F?"

Sam: "Because every time I went to
school, I passed right on by algebra
class."

What is a hunter's favorite subject?
Trigger-nometry.

Teacher: "If there are 365 days in a year
and 24 hours in a day, how many sec-
onds are there?"
Ashley: "Twelve."
Teacher: "How did you get twelve?"
Ashley: "Well, there's January second,
February second, March second. . ."

What did the circle say to the triangle?
"I'll always be around if you need me!"

Who invented fractions?
Henry the 1/8.

Teacher: "If there are seven flies on a desk and I hit one with a ruler, how many are left?"
Student: "Just the squashed one!"

✎ ✐

Teacher: If you add 28,714 and 57,935, divide the answer by 3, then multiply by 4, what do you get?"
Student: "The wrong answer!"

✎ ✐

Teacher: "Ginny, if you worked eight hours a day for three dollars an hour, what would you get?"
Ginny: "A new job."

Father: "What have you been studying in school, Priscilla?"
Priscilla: "Mostly Gozinta, Dad."
Father: "What in the world is Gozinta— a language?"

Priscilla: "No, just Gozinta. Two gozinta four, four gozinta eight. . ."

Teacher: "If I cut a steak in two, then cut the halves in two, what do I get?"
Student: "Quarters."
Teacher: "Very good. And what would I get if I cut it again?"
Student: "Eighths."
Teacher: "Great job! And if I cut it again?"
Student: "Sixteenths."
Teacher: "Wonderful! And again?"
Student: "Hamburger."

Where did King Arthur study for his math test?

In Cram-a-lot.

A little girl's teacher asked her to count to ten.

"One, two, three, four, five, six, seven, eight, ten!" she said.

"Didn't you forget something?" asked the teacher. "What about nine?"

"Well," she explained, "seven ate nine."

Teacher: "If you have fifteen potatoes and must divide them equally among five people, how would you do it?"
Shelly: "I'd mash them."

Teacher: "If you had ten dollars and your sister took two dollars, what would you have?"
Student: "A fit!"

Teacher: "What is 21 times 6?"
Student: "126."
Teacher: "That's very good."
Student: "Very good? It's *perfect!*"

Teacher: "If I bought a hundred bagels for
    a dollar, what would each bagel be?"
Student: "Stale!"

Why was the math book sad?
    Because it had so many problems.

Teacher: "Todd, if I put nineteen marbles
    in my left pocket, and twenty-three
    marbles in my right pocket, what
    would I have?"
Todd: "Heavy pants!"

Math teacher: "If you had one dollar and
you asked your father for two more,
how many would you have?"

Student: "One dollar."

Math teacher: "No. You don't know your
addition."

Student: "No. You don't know my father!"

Why did the student take her math
homework to gym class?

She wanted to work out her problems.

Son: "Dad, can you help me find the
lowest common denominator in this
problem, please?"

Father: "Don't tell me that they haven't
found it yet! I remember looking for
it when I was your age."

Math teacher: "What is a polygon?"
Student: "A dead parrot."

Teacher: "Did your parents help you with these math problems?"
Student: "No, I got them wrong all by myself."

Student: "Teacher, I can't figure out this problem."
Teacher: "Any five year old should be able to solve this one."
Student: "No wonder I can't do it then—I'm almost nine!"

The teacher was reviewing counting with her kindergarten class. "Emily," she asked, "can you count to ten without mistakes?"

"Yes," said Emily, and she did.

"Now, Evan," said the teacher, "can you count from ten to twenty?"

"With or without mistakes?" asked Evan.

❧ ✏

"What are algebraic symbols for?" a sixth grader asked her high-school sister.

"That's how the math teacher talks when he can't express himself in plain English," she answered.

The teacher asked Penny, "Can you count to ten?"

Penny answered, "Yes." She began counting on her fingers, "One, two, three, four, five, six, seven, eight, nine, ten."

"Good," the teacher praised, "now can you count higher?"

"Yes!" Penny said. She raised her

hands over her head and counted on her fingers again, "One, two, three, four, five, six, seven, eight, nine, ten."

Teacher: "If I lay one egg here and another there, how many eggs will there be?"
Student: "None."
Teacher: "Why 'none'?"
Student: "Because you can't lay eggs!"

What makes math hard work?
All those numbers you have to carry.

What kind of tree does a math teacher climb?
Geometry.

What do you have to know to get top grades in geometry?

All the angles.

What kind of pliers do you use in arithmetic?

Multipliers.

Math teacher: "If you got ten dollars from ten people, what would you have?"

Student: "A new bike."

Father: "What did you learn in school today?"

Son: "That three plus three is seven."

Father: "Three plus three is six."

Son: "Well, I guess I didn't learn anything today then."

What do math teachers eat?

Square meals.

At the beginning of math class, the teacher asked, "Timmy, what are 3 and 6 and 27 and 45?"

Timmy quickly answered, "NBC, CBS, ESPN, and the Cartoon Network!"

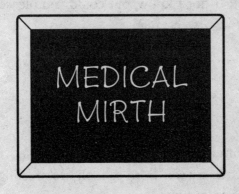

MEDICAL MIRTH

School nurse: "I'm sorry you hit your finger with a hammer! How does it feel now?"

Parker: "Smashing!"

School nurse: "How do you feel after getting hit by the baseball?"

Ivan: "Never felt batter!"

School nurse: "Why do you think you're
a bird?"
Pat: "I don't know, but could you please
just tweet me?"

✎   ✏

MEDICAL EXCUSES

From a car battery salesman: "Please
excuse my son from school. He's feeling
a bit run down."

From a chimney sweep: "Becca won't be
in school today. She caught the flue."

From a hockey player: "My daughter has
a bad case of chicken pucks."

✎   ✏

School nurse to sick girl: "What is your
name, so we can notify your parents?"
Girl: "Oh, my parents already know my
name."

"What do you plan to take for your cold?" the teacher asked Diane.

"Maybe I'll take the rest of the week off," said Diane.

Student to school nurse: "Nurse, I think
    a bee crawled inside my ear."
Nurse: "Hmm. . .you seem fine.
    What gave you that idea?"
Student: "I don't know, but it's been
    going through my head all
    morning."

Sydney: "I must have sneezed fifty times
    today. Do you think there's some-
    thing in the air?"
Allen: "Yes, your germs!"

Where is the best place to have the nurse's office at school?

Next to the cafeteria.

Teacher: "George, did you write this note that was supposed to be from your parents?"

George: "Why would you think that?"

Teacher: "Because it says, 'Please excuse George for being sick January 30, 31, 32, and 33.'"

It was time for flu vaccinations at school, and Jerry and his class went to the nurse's office to get their shots.

When it was Jerry's turn, the nurse asked, "Which arm would you like it in?"

Jerry pointed to the school bully and said, "How about his?"

What did the principal do when he discovered the weight machine was stolen from the nurse's office?

He launched a full-scale investigation.

✏ ✒

Son: "I can't go to school today, Dad."
Father: "Why not?"
Son: "I don't feel well."
Father: "Where don't you feel well?"
Son: "In school."

✏ ✒

Myles was playing at recess when he fell down and broke his right arm. Justin ran to him and said, "Wow, Myles, you're so lucky! Now you don't have to take any tests!"

"No, I'm not lucky at all," answered Myles.

"Why do you say that?" asked Justin.

"Because," said Myles, "I'm left-handed; I meant to fall on my other arm."

A schoolteacher had injured his back and had to wear a plaster cast around the upper part of his body. It was not noticeable at all under his shirt.

On the first day of school, he discovered that many of his students were unruly and disrespectful. He confidently walked to the window and opened it. He then sat at his desk and began looking at his notes. When a strong breeze made his tie flap, he took the stapler and stapled the tie to his chest.

He had no trouble with discipline that year.

Teacher on the telephone: "You say Owen has a cold and won't be coming to school today? With whom am I speaking?"

Hoarse voice: "This is my father."

MUSIC MADNESS

How did the trombone pass first grade?
The teacher let it slide.

What happened to the musical composer
who failed all his classes?
He was held Bach a year.

What has forty feet and sings?
The school choir.

Teacher: "Dana, would you take a note to
your mother?"
Dana: "Sure. How about an F-sharp?"

Teacher: "In music, if *f* means *forte,*
what does *ff* mean?"
Student: "Eighty."

Music teacher: "In a choir, there are two
male vocal parts. One is the tenor.
What is the other?"
Student: "Um, the niner?"

Why did the high-school band eat rabbit
stew for a whole week?
They wanted to play hip-hop.

What did the drummer say when his band teacher told him he had no rhythm?

"That's because I'm beat."

Why did the trombone player get kicked out of the band?

Because he kept letting things slide.

How do you make a bandstand?

Take away their chairs.

Why did the drummer bring a chicken to band practice?

He needed new drumsticks.

The high-school band was nervous. So was the new music teacher. As they were preparing for their first concert, he told the kids that if they weren't sure of their part, just to pretend to play.

When the big night arrived, the proud parents waited expectantly. The teacher brought down the baton with a flourish, and lo, the band gave forth with a resounding silence.

READING AND WRITING REPARTEE

Selected reading for the class clown:

How I Became a Genius
   by Skip A. Grade

My Favorite Time of the Day
   by Belle Rings and Rhea Sess

The Book of Confusion
   by Kay Oss Rains

How to Behave in the Classroom
   by Sid Down and Bea Quiet

Teacher: "Ella, please use the word *camphor* in a sentence."

Ella: "In the summer, my parents send me to camphor a week."

Teacher: "Max, please use the word *acquire* in a sentence."

Max: "Someday I'd like to sing in acquire."

Mr. Carter, the English teacher, asked Kim to give him a sentence with an object.

"You are an awesome teacher," replied Kim.

"Good," said Mr. Carter, "but what is the object?"

"To get an A in English," said Kim.

Teacher: "Pam, use the words *depart,*
decide, and *deface* in a sentence."
Pam: "Depart of your hair should never
hang over decide of deface."

Teacher: "Ty, did you finish reading *The*
History of Milk?"
Ty: "No, but I skimmed most of it."

Teacher: "Did you finish reading the
book about jungle animals, Becky?"
Becky: "Well, I read between the lions."

Teacher: "Bill, can you define
procrastination?"
Bill: "Yes, but not right now."

What do word lovers like for breakfast?
Scrabbled eggs.

If Samuel Clemens was cloned, we
would have identical Twains.

Teacher: "Please define *infinity.*"
Phil: "Uh, umm. . ."
Teacher: "I know you can do it."
Phil: "Uh, uh. . ."
Teacher: "Take a guess."
Phil: "Uh. . .this could take forever!"

Teacher: "What does *estimate* mean?"
Tammy: "Can I guess?"

Books for math students:

Arithmetic Problems
　　　by Troy Kant Add

Math Made Simple
　　　by Cal Q. Later

Straight Lines
　　　by Ray D. Us

Adding Large Numbers
　　　by Cary D. Wun

Teacher: "Class, who can spell *collie?*"
Chuck: "Oh no, it's another pup quiz!"

Teacher: "Ryan, please use *ransom* in a sentence."

Ryan: "Yesterday I walked some, then I ransom."

Teacher: "Samantha, define *ignorance* and *apathy*."

Samantha: "I don't know, and I don't care."

Teacher: "Use *malign* in a sentence."

Mark: "I sure hope a fish bites malign."

Teacher: "Is there anyone who can use *finite* in a sentence?"

Mikayla: "I can. It's a finite for a walk in the park."

Teacher: "Troy, use the word *migrate* in a
    sentence, please."
Troy: "Every Christmas, migrate grandma
    comes to visit."

Teacher: "What is *can't* short for?"
Student: "Cannot."
Teacher: "That's right. And what is *don't*
    short for?"
Student: "Doughnut!"

Teacher: "What does *minimum* mean?"
Student: "A very small mother."
Teacher: "Then what does *maximum*
    mean?"
Student: "A very big mother."

Teacher: "What is the longest word in
   the English language?"
Student: "Smiles—because there is a mile
   between the first and last letters."

Why shouldn't you write on an empty
stomach?
   Because paper is much better.

What letter is not in the alphabet?
   The letter I mailed this morning.

The teacher asked her students to each
write three sentences using the word *beans*.
   Nate wrote, "A farmer grows beans.
I like to eat beans. We are all human
beans."

What occurs once in a century, twice in a lifetime, but not even once in a day?

The letter e.

Teacher: "Hope, did your father write this story?"

Hope: "Well, he tried, but Mom had to do it all over again."

Teacher: "Leann, your poem was the best in the class. Did you really write it?"

Leann: "Yes. I wrote it while Mom dictated it."

Teacher: "How do you spell *inconsequentially?*"

Daniel: "Wrong."

Teacher: "What is the plural of mouse?"

Student: "Mice."

Teacher: "Good. Now, what's the plural of baby?"

Student: "Twins!"

Teacher: "What is your favorite state, Max?"

Max: "Mississippi."

Teacher: "How do you spell it?"

Max: "Um. . .I think I like Ohio much better."

English teacher: "What is the opposite of grief?"

Student: "Happiness."

Teacher: "And sadness?"

Student: "Gladness."

Teacher: "And the opposite of woe is. . . ?"

Student: "Giddyup."

Teacher: "Albert, please give me an
example of a collective noun."
Albert: "A magnet."

Teacher: "What comes after *O?*"
Ginger: "Yeah."

Teacher: "Randy, everyone else wrote a
five-page report on milk. Yours is
only one page. Why is that?"
Randy: "I wrote about condensed milk."

Teacher: "What is the longest sentence
you can think of?"
Student: "Life imprisonment."

The school board determined that speech and debate would be removed from the course schedule; there was no argument.

A teacher asked her class: "If I had eight apples in my left hand and nine apples in my right hand, what would I have?"

A voice from the back of the classroom answered, "Really big hands!"

"An abstract noun," the teacher said, "is something you can think of but you can't touch. Can you give me an example of one?"

"Yes," a boy in the junior class replied, "my father's new car."

Why can you always tell what Dick and Jane will do next?
They're so easy to read.

Where does success come before work?
In the dictionary.

Teacher: "Can you give me a sentence with the word *politics* in it?"
Student: "My parrot swallowed a watch, and now Polly ticks."

What did the pencil say to the piece of paper?
"I dot my Is on you."

Where do children learn their ABCs?
At LMN-tary school.

Kim hadn't talked to her grandparents for a while and decided she should call and update them.

"I had a terrible time!" she told them. "First off, I got tonsillitis, followed by appendicitis and pneumonia. After that, I got rheumatism, and then they gave me hypodermics and inoculations. I thought I would *never* get through that spelling bee!"

Teacher: "Name two pronouns."
Student: "Who, me?"

TIPS TO IMPROVE YOUR WRITING:

- Avoid alliteration. Always.

- Never use a long word when a diminutive one will do.

- Employ the vernacular.

- Avoid ampersands & abbreviations, etc.

- Parenthetical remarks (however relevant) are unnecessary.

- Remember to never split an infinitive.

- Contractions aren't necessary.

- Foreign words and phrases are not *apropos*.

- One should never generalize.

- Eliminate quotations. As Ralph Waldo Emerson said, "I hate quotations. Tell me what you know."

- Comparisons are as bad as cliches.

- Don't be redundant; don't use more words than necessary; it's highly superfluous.

- Be more or less specific.

- Understatement is always best.

- One-word sentences? Eliminate.

- Analogies in writing are like feathers on a snake.

- The passive voice is to be avoided.

- Go around the barn at high noon to avoid colloquialisms.

- Who needs rhetorical questions?

- Exaggeration is a billion times worse than understatement.

- Don't never use a double negation.

- Capitalize every sentence and remember always end it with a point.
- Do not put statements in the negative form.

- Verbs has to agree with their subjects.

- Poofread carefully to see if you words or letters out.

- If you reread your work, you can find on rereading, a great deal of repetition can be avoided by rereading and editing.

- A writer must not shift your point of view.

- And don't start a sentence with a conjunction. (Remember, too, a preposition is a terrible word to end a sentence with.)

- Don't overuse exclamation marks!!!

- Place pronouns as close as possible, especially in long sentences, as of ten or more words, to the antecedents.

- Writing carefully, dangling participles must be avoided.

- If any word is improper at the end of a sentence, a linking verb is.

- Take the bull by the hand and avoid mixing metaphors.

- Avoid trendy locutions that sound flaky.

- Every person should be careful to use

a singular pronoun with singular nouns in their writing.

- The adverb always follows the verb.

- Last but not least, avoid cliches like the plague; they're old hat; seek viable alternatives.

SCIENCE SILLIES

Teacher: "What family does the octopus belong to?"
Student: "Nobody's that I know."

A teacher had just discussed magnets with her class. A bit later, she said, "My name begins with *M*, and I pick things up. What am I?"

Niles thought for a moment and answered, "Mom!"

Teacher: "Can anyone give me the name
of a liquid that won't freeze?"
Lynn: "Hot water."

Teacher: "Can anyone tell me what the
Dog Star is?"
Student: "Lassie."

Teacher: "Do we get fur from a grizzly
bear?"
Student: "I'd get as fur from him as
possible!"

Science teacher: "Who can tell me how
far light travels?"
Cheryl: "I'm not sure, but it gets to my
house very early in the morning."

Teacher: "Where are elephants found?"
Student: "I don't know. They're so big I
    didn't think they could get lost!"

Teacher: "What is the difference between
    electricity and lightning?"
Student: "Lightning is free."

The students in the chemistry class were
watching the professor give a demonstra-
tion of the properties of various acids.
"Now," said the professor, "I am going to
drop a silver dollar into this glass of acid.
Will it dissolve?"

"No, sir," answered one of the
students.

"No?" quizzed the professor. "Could
you explain to the class why it won't
dissolve?"

"Because," the student replied, "if the money would dissolve, then you wouldn't drop it in."

✎ ✐

Teacher: "Why does the Statue of Liberty stand in New York harbor?"
Jerry: "Because it can't sit down."

✎ ✐

THE FOLLOWING ARE ANSWERS TO FIFTH-GRADE SCIENCE EXAMS:

H_2O is hot water, and CO_2 is cold water.

Nitrogen is not found in Ireland because it is not found in a free state.

To collect fumes of sulfur, hold a deacon over a flame in a test tube.

A fossil is an extinct animal. The older it is, the more extinct it is.

When you smell an odorless gas, it is probably carbon monoxide.

Three kinds of blood vessels are arteries, vanes, and caterpillars.

Vacuum: A large, empty space where the pope lives.

The moon is a planet just like Earth, only it is even deader.

Dew is formed on leaves when the sun shines down on them and makes them perspire.

A supersaturated solution is one that holds more than it can hold.

Mushrooms always grow in damp places and so they look like umbrellas.

The pistol of a flower is its only protection against insects.

Respiration is composed of two acts: first inspiration and then expectoration.

The alimentary canal is located in the northern part of Indiana.

When you breathe, you inspire. When you do not breath, you expire.

The skeleton is what is left after the insides have been taken out and the outsides have been taken off. The purpose of the skeleton is something to hitch meat to.

The tides are a fight between the earth and the moon. All water tends towards the moon, because there is no water in the moon, and nature abhors a vacuum. I forget where the sun joins the fight.

Equator: A menagerie lion running around Earth through Africa.

Germinate: To become a naturalized German.

Liter: A nest of young puppies.

Momentum: What you give a person when they are going away.

Planet: A body of Earth surrounded by sky.

Rhubarb: A kind of celery gone bloodshot.

Blood flows down one leg and up the other.

A permanent set of teeth consists of eight canines, eight cuspids, two molars, and eight cuspidors.

Before giving a blood transfusion, find out if the blood is affirmative or negative.

For a nosebleed: Put the nose much lower then the body until the heart stops.

For asphyxiation: Apply artificial respiration until the patient is dead.

For a head cold: Use an agonizer to spray the nose until it drops in your throat.

To keep milk from turning sour: Keep it in the cow.

✎ ✏

Chemistry teacher: "What is the formula for water?"
Student: "H, I, J, K, L, M, N, O."
Chemistry teacher: "What kind of answer is that?"
Student: "You said it was H to O!"

A teacher was teaching about the circulation of the blood. Trying to explain it further, he said, "If I stood on my head, the blood, as you know, would run into it, and I would turn red in the face. Then why is it that while I am standing upright in the ordinary position, the blood doesn't run into my feet?"

A young boy responded, "It's because your feet aren't empty."

Teacher: "What happens to gold when it is exposed to the air?"
Student: "It gets stolen?"

Teacher: "How can you prove the world is round?"
Student: "I didn't say it was!"

Teacher: "Why is television called a 'medium'?"
Student: "Because it isn't rare or well done."

SOCIAL STUDIES SNICKERS

Teacher: "Which is farther away, Australia or the moon?"

Dave: "Australia. You can see the moon at night."

Teacher: "Who can tell me which month has 28 days?"

Chris: "All of them!"

Teacher: "Where are the kings and
    queens of England crowned?"
Hilary: "On their heads."

What language do they speak in Cuba?
    Cubic.

Teacher: "Amy, please name the four
    seasons."
Amy: "Salt, pepper, mustard, and vinegar."

After a lesson on weather in the month
of March, the teacher asked her class,
"What is it that comes in like a lion and
goes out like a lamb?"

    A student answered, "My dad."

A first-grade teacher told her class that nowadays more twins are born than in the past. One little boy asked, "Why is that?"

Before the teacher could answer, another little boy said, "Because these days, kids are afraid to come into the world alone!"

"Who invented the bow and arrow?" asked the teacher.

"Cavemen!" Gary called out enthusiastically.

"Cavemen? And what do you suppose prompted cavemen to come up with the bow and arrow?"

"Uh. . .somebody kept stealing the wheel?"

Teacher: "What can we do to stop pol-
    luting our waters?"
Student: "Stop taking baths."

SPORTS SMIRKS

Dad: "Jack, I heard you went out for the
football team!"

Jack: "Yes. . .the coach sent me out to get
the pizzas."

Boy: "Coach, why does that guy
look so mad when he runs
a marathon?"

Coach: "He's a cross-country runner."

The soccer team was losing badly. In desperation, the coach ran over to his worst player and said, "Chad, I want you to go out there and get mean and tough!"

"Okay, Coach!" said Chad. He jumped to his feet and, looking at the other team's players, asked, "Uh, Coach, which one's Mean and which one's Tough?"

What do you call a one-hundred-year-old cheerleader?
Old Yeller.

Little League coach: "What would you do if it was the bottom of the ninth with two outs and three runners on base?"
Relief pitcher: "I'd come out of the dugout so I could see better!"

A star high-school quarterback had let his schoolwork slide, and the conference championship game was quickly approaching. His coach begged the school superintendent to let the boy play. With the coach's continued persistence, the superintendent agreed. "Bring your player into my office. I'll give him a short quiz. If he passes, he will be permitted to play. If not, you'll have to play the game without him."

The coach went to get the player and quickly returned. "What is seven plus five?" asked the superintendent.

The quarterback thought for a moment, then answered, "Eleven."

The coach's face turned white. "Please, give him another chance!" he begged. "He only missed it by two!"

Why did the baseball player take his bat to the library?

His teacher told him to hit the books.

✎　✏

What is a runner's favorite subject in school?

Jog-raphy.

✎　✏

A college crew team had spent the whole afternoon rowing and were exhausted. As they headed toward the locker room, the team captain stopped them.

"Guys, I have some good news and some bad news," he began. "The good news is you can take a twenty-minute break, and then the college president is coming down here to watch you perform."

The rowers groaned. "And what's the bad news?" one asked sarcastically.

"He's bringing along his water skis."

Why does someone who runs marathons make a good student?

Because education pays off in the long run.

STAFF
SMILES

One day, while out at recess, two boys
noticed that a van began rolling down the
parking lot with no one in the driver's
seat. They quickly ran to the vehicle,
jumped in, and put on the emergency
brake. Seconds later, the door opened and
there was the principal, his face red with
anger. "What's going on?" he demanded.

"We stopped this van from rolling
away," said one of the boys.

The principal, huffing and sweaty,
said, "I know. It stalled, and I was push-
ing it."

The mother said, "Son, it's time to get up and go to school."

"Mom, nobody likes me in school. The teachers don't like me. The kids don't like me. The superintendent wants to transfer me. The bus drivers can't stand me, the school board wants me to quit, and I don't want to go to school!"

His mother sternly replied, "Son, you must go to school. You are healthy, you have a lot to learn, and a lot to teach others. You are a leader. And besides," she added, "you're forty-six years old, and you're the principal!"

The new principal was walking through the halls, preparing for the first day of school, which was only four days away. Passing the stockroom, he was surprised to see the door wide open and teachers hurrying in and out, carrying off books and supplies.

The school where he had been principal the previous year had used a check-out system only slightly less elaborate than that at Fort Knox.

Cautiously, he whispered to the custodian, "Do you think it's wise to keep the stockroom door unlocked and allow the teachers to take things without requisitions?"

The custodian looked at him for a moment, then whispered back, "We trust them with the children, don't we?"

Teacher: "There will only be a half day of school this morning."

Students: "Hooray!"

Teacher: "Then we'll have the other half this afternoon."

Josh went to the teachers' lounge and knocked on the door. "Did anyone lose twenty dollars attached to a rubber band?" he asked.

"Oh, yes, I did," said one of the teachers.

"Well, I've got great news for you," said Josh. "I found the rubber band!"

On the last day of school, one teacher said to another, "You should have heard all of the excitement. When the last bell rang, everyone clapped their hands, stomped their feet, and shouted with joy."

"It was pretty crazy, wasn't it?" replied the second teacher.

"It sure was!" said the first. "And that was just in the teachers' lounge!"

Why did the teacher wear sunglasses?
Because his class was so bright.

Did you hear about the cross-eyed
teacher?
He couldn't control his pupils.

Teacher: "Do you like to come to school,
   Daniel?"
Daniel: "Yes, and I like to go home, too.
   It's the in-between time that I don't
   really like."

Teacher: "You can't sleep in my class!"
Bobbie: "I think I could if you didn't
   speak so loud."

A kindergarten teacher was having a difficult time putting each child's boots on after a very rainy morning. After some hard tugging, she finally got Barry's on his feet when he said, "These aren't mine."

The frustrated teacher had to pull hard to remove them from the little boy's feet. She sat down next to him and asked, "So, whose boots are these?"

Barry answered, "They're my brother's, but my mom lets me wear them."

Teacher: "Why do you have cotton balls in your ear? Do you have an infection?"

Student: "No. I'm just trying to keep everything you say from going in one ear and out the other."

To be a first-grade teacher, you have to have skill, dedication, and an immunity to knock-knock jokes.

Why did the teacher put rubber bands on her students' heads?

So they could make snap decisions.

Teacher: "Class, someone has taken my purse. It had one hundred dollars in it. You're all pretty good kids, so I'll give a ten-dollar reward to whoever returns it."

A voice from the back of the room said, "I'm offering twenty dollars!"

A first-grade teacher collected some old, well-known proverbs. She gave each child in her class the first half of a proverb and had them complete the rest:

As you shall make your bed so shall you. . . mess it up.

Better be safe than. . .punch a fifth grader.

Strike while the. . .bug is close.

It's always darkest before. . .Daylight Savings Time.

You can lead a horse to water but. . .how?

Don't bite the hand that. . .looks dirty.

A miss is as good as a. . .Mr.

You can't teach an old dog new. . .math.

If you lie down with the dogs, you'll. . .
stink in the morning.

The pen is mightier than the. . .pigs.

An idle mind is. . .the best way to relax.

Where there's smoke, there's. . .pollution.

Happy the bride who. . .gets all the
presents.

A penny saved is. . .not much.

Two's company, three's. . .the musketeers.

Laugh and the whole world laughs with
you, cry and. . .you have to blow your
nose.

Children should be seen and not. . .
spanked or grounded.

When the blind leadeth the blind. . .get
out of the way.

The school pictures were taken, and the
teacher was trying to encourage the
students each to buy a copy of the group
picture. "Just think how great it will be to
look at it when you are all grown up and
say, 'There's Michael; he's a lawyer,' or
'That's Phyllis; she's a doctor.' "

A small voice from the back of the
room called out, "And there's Mrs.
Dobson; she's still old and wrinkled."

Just before Christmas, the kindergarten
teacher was inundated with gifts.

The florist's daughter presented her
with a gift. She shook it, held it over her
head, and said, "I think I can guess what

it is—some flowers!"

"You're right!" said the little girl. "But how did you know?"

"Oh, it was just a guess," she said with a smile.

The next student was a candy store owner's son. The teacher held the gift over her head, shook it, and said, "I think I can guess what this is—a box of candy!"

"That's right! But how did you know that?" asked the boy.

"Oh, just another good guess," said the teacher, smiling.

The next gift was from a little boy whose father managed the local cola bottling company. When the teacher picked up the box, it began leaking. She smiled and asked the boy, "Is it orange soda?"

"Noo," the boy replied.

The teacher tried again: "Is it lemon-lime soda?" she asked.

"Noo," the boy answered.

The teacher then said, "Well, I can't

guess this one. I give up; what is it?"

The boy replied, "It's a puppy!"

Every year, the teacher sent a note home with each child that read, "Dear Parents, if you promise not to believe everything your child says happens at school, I'll promise not to believe everything he or she says happens at home."

Finding one of her students making faces at other children on the playground, Miss Green gently corrected the boy, "When I was your age, I was told if I made a scary face, it might stay that way."

The little boy looked at her and said, "Well, you can't say you weren't warned!"

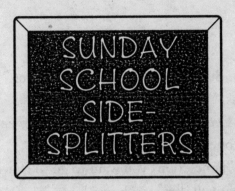

SUNDAY
SCHOOL
SIDE-
SPLITTERS

A Sunday school teacher asked her fifth-grade class which events in the life of Jesus impressed them the most and which happenings they liked the best. These were some of the responses:

"When Jesus raised Lazarus from the dead."

"When He raised the twelve-year-old girl to life."

"When He helped the apostles catch so many fish that their boat began to sink."

But Frank's response was, "I like the

story about the big crowd that loafs and fishes."

The Sunday school teacher asked her class, "Who wants to go to heaven?"

Everyone held up their hands except for one young boy.

"James, don't you want to go to heaven when you die?"

"Oh, yes, when I die, but I thought you were getting a bunch to go now."

A father was teaching his son to admire the beauty in nature.

"Look, Will," he exclaimed, "isn't that a beautiful sunset that God painted?"

"It sure is, Dad," he agreed, "especially since God had to paint it with His left hand."

The father was bewildered. "What do you mean—His left hand?"

"Well," he said, "my Sunday school teacher said that Jesus is sitting on God's right hand."

The Sunday school teacher, trying to get a response from his class of eight-year-old boys, said, "Boys, can't you imagine Noah, on that ark, spending a lot of time fishing?"

One boy replied, "I don't think he did. He only had two worms!"

Little boy's prayer: "Dear God, please take care of my mommy and daddy and sister and grandma and grandpa. And please God, take care of Yourself, or else we're all sunk!"

Sunday school teacher: "Taylor, do you
disobey your parents?"

Taylor: "No, sir."

Sunday school teacher: "Do you ever use
mean words?"

Taylor: "No, sir."

Sunday school teacher: "You must do
something wrong every once in a
while!"

Taylor: "Well, I don't always tell the
truth."

✎ ✐

A teacher asked her kindergarten class,
"Can a bear take his warm coat off?"

"No," they all answered.

"Why not?"

There was a long silence. Finally, a
young boy spoke up, "Because only God
knows where the buttons are."

A Sunday school class was reviewing the lesson of Jonah. "What is it that we can learn from the story of Jonah and the whale?" asked the teacher.

One student replied, "People make whales sick!"

❧ ✏

Sunday school teacher: "Gretchen, what can you tell me about Goliath?"
Gretchen: "Goliath was the man David rocked to sleep."

❧ ✏

Dustin listened attentively to the Sunday school lesson about the parable of the Prodigal Son.

"And what happened when the Prodigal Son returned home?" asked the teacher at the end of the lesson.

"His father went to meet him and

hurt himself," replied Dustin.

"Hurt himself?" asked the teacher. "Where did you learn that?"

"From the Bible," answered Dustin. "It says his father ran to meet him and fell on his neck."

✎ ✏

At Sunday school, Mr. Duncan told his students that God created everything, including human beings. Freddy seemed especially intent when Mr. Duncan explained that Eve was created out of one of Adam's ribs.

Later in the week, his mother noticed him lying on the floor and asked, "Freddy, what is the matter?"

Freddy responded, "I have a pain in my side. I think I'm gonna have a wife."

The Sunday school teacher was explaining the story of Elijah and the false prophets of Baal. She explained how Elijah built the altar, put wood on it, cut the steer in pieces, and laid it upon the altar. Then Elijah commanded the people of God to fill four barrels of water and pour them over the altar. He had them do this four times.

"Can anyone tell me why God would ask Elijah to pour water over the steer on the altar?" asked the teacher.

A little girl excitedly answered, "To make the gravy!"

The Sunday school teacher was telling his class the story of the Prodigal Son. Attempting to emphasize the bitterness of the elder brother, he stressed that part of the parable.

After describing how the household

rejoiced over the return of the wayward son, the teacher spoke of one who failed to share in the joyful spirit. "Can anyone tell me who this was?" he asked the class.

"I know! I know!" a young girl responded. "It was the fattened calf."

A little boy had just gotten home from Sunday school. While his mother was cooking lunch, he asked, "Is it true that before you're born you're just dust and after you die you go back to being dust?"

"Yes, Son. Why do you ask?"

"Well, that's what my Sunday school teacher said today."

"Yes, she's right. Now go on and wash your hands. Lunch will be ready in a few minutes."

About ten minutes later, she called for him to come for lunch. As they were sitting down to eat, the little boy asked again about being dust before you're born and after you die. Once again, the mother informed her son that it was true.

The little boy looked at her and said, "Then you'd better go to my room pretty quick, because something under my bed is either coming or going!"

Definitions given by children in a Sunday school class:

Conversion: "The point after a touchdown."

Fast Days: "The days you have to eat in a hurry."

Epistle: "The wife of an apostle."

"I used to think that King David was a hero, but I don't think that anymore," declared Bobby after Sunday school.

"Why not, Bobby?" asked his mother.

"I found out today that he killed the Jolly Green Giant."

✎ ✐

A Sunday school class was learning John 3:16. One child recited it, "For God so loved the world that He gave His only begotten Son, that whosoever believeth in Him should not perish, but have ever-laughing life."

✎ ✐

Toward the end of Sunday school one morning, a little boy asked the teacher, "Are there animals in heaven?"

"What kind of animals?" the teacher asked.

"Animals—like cows and bees," said the boy.

"Well, I'm not sure," answered the teacher, "but I don't think they'll be necessary in heaven."

"But then where will we get enough milk and honey for everybody?" he asked.

✎ ✐

A Sunday school teacher was reading a Bible story to her class, "The man named Lot was warned to take his wife and flee out of the city, but his wife looked back and turned to salt."

A little boy asked softly, "What happened to the flea?"

✎ ✐

"Wasn't it good that the shepherds put on clean clothes before they went to see baby Jesus?" asked the little boy.

His mother questioned, "How do you know they did that?"

"Well," he replied, "in Sunday school we sang 'While Shepherds Washed Their Socks by Night.'"

✎ ✏

Sunday school teacher: "What became of Tyre?"
Student: "God punctured it."

✎ ✏

A Sunday school teacher was trying to convey the message of the story of the Good Samaritan. Finally, she asked, "Betsy, suppose you passed an empty lot and saw a man in ragged clothes lying on the ground, badly beaten up, and covered with blood. What would you do?"

The young girl answered, "I think I would throw up."

A Sunday school teacher was discussing the Ten Commandments with her five year olds. After explaining the commandment that teaches us to "honor thy father and thy mother," she asked, "Is there a commandment that teaches us how we should treat our brothers and sisters?"

One little boy quickly answered, "Thou shalt not kill."

At Christmastime, the Sunday school teacher asked her students to draw pictures of the Nativity. The children all drew wonderful pictures, variations of the same basic scene—Mary and Joseph, baby Jesus in the manger, the animals, the shepherds, and the wise men.

The teacher was somewhat confused by little Katie's picture, though. "What is that large box in front of everyone with the lines coming out from the top?" she asked Katie.

"Oh," she answered, "that's their TV!"

❧   ✍

Rebecca went to her Sunday school teacher after class. She asked, "If the people of Israel were Israelites, and the people of Canaan were Canaanites, do we call the people from Paris parasites?"

❧   ✍

A young boy walked into his Sunday school class late. His teacher knew that he was usually very prompt so she asked, "Ryan, is something wrong?"

The boy replied, "No. I wanted to go fishing, but my dad told me that I needed to go to church."

The teacher was very impressed and asked Ryan if his dad had explained to him why it was more important to go to church than to go fishing.

Ryan answered, "Yes. Dad said he didn't have enough bait for both of us."

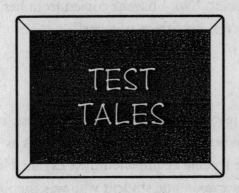

TEST
TALES

Ted: "Yea! The teacher said we'd have a
    test today, rain or shine."
Vinny: "What's so great about that?"
Ted: "It's snowing!"

Teacher: "Robert, I hope I didn't see you
    looking at Denise's paper."
Robert: "I hope you didn't, either!"

Teacher: "Robert, were you just copying
    Jayne's answers?"
Robert: "No, I haven't copied from her
    test for fifteen minutes!"

✎   ✐

A teacher was giving a true/false test. He
was walking up and down the aisles as
the students completed their exams. He
came upon one student who was flipping
a coin, then writing.

"What are you doing?" the teacher
asked.

"Getting the answers to the test,"
replied the student.

The teacher shook his head and continued walking.

When everyone was finished with the
test, the teacher noticed the student was
again flipping the coin.

"Now what are you doing?" he asked.

"Oh, I'm just checking the answers."

Why did the student put on lipstick and eye shadow during class?

Because the teacher said she was giving the class a makeup test.

Teacher: "You copied from Sid's test, didn't you?"
Student: "How did you know?"
Teacher: "Sid's paper says, 'I don't know,' and you wrote, 'Me neither.'"

Father: "How were the test questions?"
Son: "Easy."
Father: "Then why do you look so unhappy?"
Son: "The questions didn't give me any trouble, just the answers."

Teacher: "Were you copying Sam's answers?"

Student: "No, I was just seeing if he got mine right."

MORE
SCHOOL
JOKES

Tom: "How are you doing in wood-carving class?"

Tim: "I'm getting better whittle by whittle."

Fran: "How do you like needlecraft?"

Nan: "I like it up to a point."

What did the gum say to the school desk?

"*I'm stuck on you!*"

"My daughter thinks she's a parachute," Mrs. Matthews told the school guidance counselor.

"Have you tried talking with her?" asked the counselor.

"I have tried," said Mrs. Matthews, "but she just won't open up."

Hal: "How did you like the magician at assembly?"

Frank: "He wasn't very good, but the teacher he sawed in half was terrific!"

Ginnie: "What are you going to do for the school talent show?"

Lori: "My imitation of a bird."

Ginnie: "What do you have planned?"

Lori: "Nothing. I think I'll just wing it."

Mother: "How did you do on your first day of school?"

Alexis: "Not very good. I have to go back again tomorrow."

Terry: "I finally made it out of eighth grade!"

Joel: "What happened?"

Terry: "We had a fire drill."

Teacher: "Keith, did you lose your train of thought?"

Keith: "No, but I think one of the cars just derailed."

✏︎ ✏︎

Hugh: "What are you going to be when you get out of school?"

George: "An old man!"

✏︎ ✏︎

Miss Williams, the fourth-grade teacher, came in from recess and asked her class, "Did anyone lose a dollar on the playground?"

A hand went up in the back of the room. "I did, Miss Williams," said Zack. "A dollar bill fell out of my pocket."

"But this was four quarters," said Miss Williams.

"Oh," replied Zack, "it must have broken when it hit the pavement."

Teacher: "What do you want to get out
of school most?"
Greg: "Me."

✎　✐

School is where you always try to do
your best—except when your friends are
watching.

✎　✐

What kind of school does Sherlock
Holmes attend?
Elementary, my dear Watson.

✎　✐

A teacher came outside to find one of
her students playing in a huge mud pud-
dle. "What are you doing?" she asked.
　The young boy looked at her and
said, "They say it rained an inch and a

quarter last night, and I really could use the quarter!"

When his son came home after his first day of school, the father asked him, "Son, what did you do at school today?"

The little boy shrugged his shoulders and said, "Not much."

Hoping to encourage his son to talk about his day, the father persisted and said, "Well, did you learn about any numbers or letters or colors?"

The child looked at his father with a bit of a confused look. "Daddy," he asked, "didn't you go to school when you were a little boy?"

Carolyn began a job as an elementary-school counselor, and she was eager to help. One day during recess, she noticed a girl standing by herself on one side of a playing field while the rest of the kids enjoyed a game of soccer at the other end.

Carolyn approached and asked the girl if she was all right. The girl said she was.

A little while later, however, Carolyn noticed the girl was in the same spot, still all alone.

Approaching her again, Carolyn asked, "Would you like me to be your friend?"

The girl hesitated, then said, "Okay," eyeing the woman suspiciously.

Feeling she was making progress, Carolyn ventured, "Why are you standing here all alone?"

"Because," the girl said, becoming slightly annoyed, "I'm the goalie!"

Teacher: "You missed school yesterday."
Student: "Well, not very much."

Father: "I hear you skipped school to
    play football."
Son: "No, I didn't, and I have the fish to
    prove it."

The brain is a wonderful thing. It starts
working the second you get up in the
morning and never stops until you are
asked a question in class.

Father: "When I was your age, I thought
    nothing of walking five miles to
    school."
Son: "I don't think much of it myself."

Teacher: "Be sure that you go straight home."

Student: "I can't; I live just around the corner."

Teacher: "When do you like school most?"

Student: "When it's closed!"

Teacher: "Luke, you try my patience!"

Luke: "No, teacher, you had better try mine. There's more of it."

Teacher: "This note from your father looks like your handwriting."

Student: "Well, he borrowed my pen."

Teacher: "I wish you would pay a little attention."

Student: "I'm paying as little as I can."

FROM A CHILD'S PERSPECTIVE

"Never sass a teacher whose eyes and ears are twitching."

—Andrew, age 9

"When you get a bad grade in school, show it to your mom when she's on the phone."

—Aleysha, age 13

"Beware of cafeteria food when it looks like it's moving."

—Rob, age 10

For several weeks, a six-year-old boy kept telling his teacher about the baby that was expected at his house.

One day, his mother put his hand on her tummy so that he could feel the movements of the unborn baby. He didn't say a word and even stopped talking to his teacher about it.

Several days later, the teacher asked him about the expected event. He began to cry and said, "I think Mommy ate it."

The kindergarten class was discussing Christmas gift ideas for their families.

"Lucy, what will you be giving your brother?" asked the teacher.

"I don't know," replied Lucy.

"Well, what did you give him last year?" she inquired.

"Chicken pox."

Father: "Are you in the top half of your class?"
Son: "No, I'm one of the students who make the top half possible."

✎ ✐

Teacher: "What is your name?"
Student: "Kyle."
Teacher: "You should say 'Sir.' "
Student: "Okay—Sir Kyle."

✎ ✐

Just before the Thanksgiving holiday, the teacher asked her kindergarten class, "What are you thankful for?"

One child answered, "I'm thankful I'm not a turkey!"

On the first day of school, a little boy handed his new teacher a note from his mother. The teacher opened the note, read it, looked at the boy, and then put the note inside her desk.

"So what does it say?" the little boy wanted to know.

"It's a disclaimer," the teacher replied.

"A what?"

"It says, 'The opinions expressed by Chris are not necessarily those of his mother and father.' "

If you enjoyed

The Teacher, Teacher Joke Book, look for these
other hilarious titles from Barbour Publishing!

*500 Clean Jokes
and Humorous Stories*
ISBN 1-57748-244-1
336 pages, $2.97

Noah's Favorite Animal Jokes
ISBN 1-58660-995-5
240 pages, $2.97

*The Ultimate Guide
to Good Clean Humor*
ISBN 1-57748-730-3
448 pages, $6.97

*The World's Greatest Collection
of Knock-Knock Jokes*
ISBN 1-55748-650-6
112 pages, $2.97

Available wherever Christian books are sold.